IOO FAVOURITE GERMAN STELLPLATZ

MOTORHOME JOURNAL

BELONGS TO

NAME ....

E MAIL ....

MOBILE ....

BLOG ....

PLEASE RETURN IF FOUND

www.fyneeditions.co.uk

MY 100 FAVOURITE
GERMAN STELLPLATZ

DATE .... ARRIVAL TIME ....

AIRE NAME ....

ADDRESS 1 ....

ADDRESS 2 ....

REGION ....

WHAT3WORDS ///...

GPS ....

COST PER NIGHT € .... RECOMMEND – YES / NO

NO. OF NIGHTS HERE .... WEATHER ....

FACILITIES   THINGS TO SEE / DO LOCALLY

YES / NO – ELECTRICITY   ....

YES / NO – FRESH WATER   ....

YES / NO – BLACK WATER   ....

YES / NO – GREY WATER   ....

YES / NO – HARDSTANDING   ....

YES / NO – GRASS   ....

YES / NO – WI-FI   ....

NOTES

....
....
....
....
....
....
....
....
....
....
....

MY 100 FAVOURITE
GERMAN STELLPLATZ

DATE .... ARRIVAL TIME ....

AIRE NAME ....

ADDRESS 1 ....

ADDRESS 2 ....

REGION ....

WHAT3WORDS ///..

GPS ....

COST PER NIGHT € .... RECOMMEND - YES / NO

NO. OF NIGHTS HERE .... WEATHER ....

FACILITIES

THINGS TO SEE / DO LOCALLY

YES / NO - ELECTRICITY

YES / NO - FRESH WATER

YES / NO - BLACK WATER

YES / NO - GREY WATER

YES / NO - HARDSTANDING

YES / NO - GRASS

YES / NO - WI-FI

NOTES

MY 100 FAVOURITE
GERMAN STELLPLATZ

DATE .... ARRIVAL TIME ....

AIRE NAME ....

ADDRESS 1 ....

ADDRESS 2 ....

REGION ....

WHAT3WORDS ///..

GPS ....

COST PER NIGHT € .... RECOMMEND - YES / NO

NO. OF NIGHTS HERE .... WEATHER ....

FACILITIES	THINGS TO SEE / DO LOCALLY
YES / NO - ELECTRICITY	....
	....
YES / NO - FRESH WATER	....
	....
YES / NO - BLACK WATER	....
	....
YES / NO - GREY WATER	....
	....
YES / NO - HARDSTANDING	....
	....
YES / NO - GRASS	....
	....
YES / NO - WI-FI	....

NOTES

....
....
....
....
....
....
....
....
....
....
....
....

MY 100 FAVOURITE
GERMAN STELLPLATZ

DATE .... ARRIVAL TIME ....

AIRE NAME ....

ADDRESS 1 ....

ADDRESS 2 ....

REGION ....

WHAT3WORDS ///...

GPS ....

COST PER NIGHT € .... RECOMMEND - YES / NO

NO. OF NIGHTS HERE .... WEATHER ....

FACILITIES   THINGS TO SEE / DO LOCALLY

YES / NO - ELECTRICITY   ....

YES / NO - FRESH WATER   ....

YES / NO - BLACK WATER   ....

YES / NO - GREY WATER   ....

YES / NO - HARDSTANDING   ....

YES / NO - GRASS   ....

YES / NO - WI-FI   ....

NOTES

....
....
....
....
....
....
....
....
....
....
....

MY 100 FAVOURITE
GERMAN STELLPLATZ

DATE .... ARRIVAL TIME ....

AIRE NAME ....

ADDRESS 1 ....

ADDRESS 2 ....

REGION ....

WHAT3WORDS ///..

GPS ....

COST PER NIGHT € .... RECOMMEND - YES / NO

NO. OF NIGHTS HERE .... WEATHER ....

FACILITIES   THINGS TO SEE / DO LOCALLY

YES / NO - ELECTRICITY

YES / NO - FRESH WATER

YES / NO - BLACK WATER

YES / NO - GREY WATER

YES / NO - HARDSTANDING

YES / NO - GRASS

YES / NO - WI-FI

NOTES

MY 100 FAVOURITE
GERMAN STELLPLATZ

DATE .... ARRIVAL TIME ....

AIRE NAME ....

ADDRESS 1 ....

ADDRESS 2 ....

REGION ....

WHAT3WORDS ///...

GPS ....

COST PER NIGHT € .... RECOMMEND - YES / NO

NO. OF NIGHTS HERE .... WEATHER ....

FACILITIES

THINGS TO SEE / DO LOCALLY

YES / NO - ELECTRICITY

YES / NO - FRESH WATER

YES / NO - BLACK WATER

YES / NO - GREY WATER

YES / NO - HARDSTANDING

YES / NO - GRASS

YES / NO - WI-FI

....
....
....
....
....
....
....
....
....
....

NOTES

....
....
....
....
....
....
....
....
....
....
....
....
....

MY 100 FAVOURITE
GERMAN STELLPLATZ

DATE .... ARRIVAL TIME ....

AIRE NAME ....

ADDRESS 1 ....

ADDRESS 2 ....

REGION ....

WHAT3WORDS ///...

GPS ....

COST PER NIGHT € .... RECOMMEND – YES / NO

NO. OF NIGHTS HERE .... WEATHER ....

FACILITIES   THINGS TO SEE / DO LOCALLY

YES / NO - ELECTRICITY   ....
                              ....
YES / NO - FRESH WATER   ....
                              ....
YES / NO - BLACK WATER   ....
                              ....
YES / NO - GREY WATER   ....
                              ....
YES / NO - HARDSTANDING   ....
                              ....
YES / NO - GRASS   ....
                              ....
YES / NO - WI-FI   ....

NOTES

....
....
....
....
....
....
....
....
....
....
....
....

MY 100 FAVOURITE GERMAN STELLPLATZ

DATE .... ARRIVAL TIME ....

AIRE NAME ....

ADDRESS 1 ....

ADDRESS 2 ....

REGION ....

WHAT3WORDS ///...

GPS ....

COST PER NIGHT € .... RECOMMEND - YES / NO

NO. OF NIGHTS HERE .... WEATHER ....

FACILITIES

YES / NO - ELECTRICITY

YES / NO - FRESH WATER

YES / NO - BLACK WATER

YES / NO - GREY WATER

YES / NO - HARDSTANDING

YES / NO - GRASS

YES / NO - WI-FI

THINGS TO SEE / DO LOCALLY

....
....
....
....
....
....
....
....
....
....

NOTES

....
....
....
....
....
....
....
....
....
....
....

MY 100 FAVOURITE GERMAN STELLPLATZ

DATE .... ARRIVAL TIME ....

AIRE NAME ....

ADDRESS 1 ....

ADDRESS 2 ....

REGION ....

WHAT3WORDS ///..

GPS ....

COST PER NIGHT € .... RECOMMEND - YES / NO

NO. OF NIGHTS HERE .... WEATHER ....

FACILITIES   THINGS TO SEE / DO LOCALLY

YES / NO - ELECTRICITY   ....

YES / NO - FRESH WATER   ....

YES / NO - BLACK WATER   ....

YES / NO - GREY WATER   ....

YES / NO - HARDSTANDING   ....

YES / NO - GRASS   ....

YES / NO - WI-FI   ....

NOTES

....
....
....
....
....
....
....
....
....
....

MY 100 FAVOURITE
GERMAN STELLPLATZ

DATE .... ARRIVAL TIME ....

AIRE NAME ....

ADDRESS I ....

ADDRESS 2 ....

REGION ....

WHAT3WORDS ///...

GPS ....

COST PER NIGHT € .... RECOMMEND - YES / NO

NO. OF NIGHTS HERE .... WEATHER ....

FACILITIES

YES / NO - ELECTRICITY

YES / NO - FRESH WATER

YES / NO - BLACK WATER

YES / NO - GREY WATER

YES / NO - HARDSTANDING

YES / NO - GRASS

YES / NO - WI-FI

THINGS TO SEE / DO LOCALLY

....
....
....
....
....
....
....
....
....
....

NOTES

....
....
....
....
....
....
....
....
....
....
....

MY 100 FAVOURITE
GERMAN STELLPLATZ

DATE .... ARRIVAL TIME ....

AIRE NAME ....

ADDRESS 1 ....

ADDRESS 2 ....

REGION ....

WHAT3WORDS ///..

GPS ....

COST PER NIGHT € .... RECOMMEND - YES / NO

NO. OF NIGHTS HERE .... WEATHER ....

FACILITIES · · · · · · · · · · · · · · · · THINGS TO SEE / DO LOCALLY

YES / NO - ELECTRICITY

....

....

YES / NO - FRESH WATER

....

....

YES / NO - BLACK WATER

....

....

YES / NO - GREY WATER

....

....

YES / NO - HARDSTANDING

....

....

YES / NO - GRASS

....

....

YES / NO - WI-FI

....

NOTES

....
....
....
....
....
....
....
....
....
....
....
....
....

MY 100 FAVOURITE
GERMAN STELLPLATZ

DATE .... ARRIVAL TIME ....

AIRE NAME ....

ADDRESS 1 ....

ADDRESS 2 ....

REGION ....

WHAT3WORDS ///...

GPS ....

COST PER NIGHT € .... RECOMMEND - YES / NO

NO. OF NIGHTS HERE .... WEATHER ....

FACILITIES   THINGS TO SEE / DO LOCALLY

YES / NO - ELECTRICITY   ....

YES / NO - FRESH WATER   ....

YES / NO - BLACK WATER   ....

YES / NO - GREY WATER   ....

YES / NO - HARDSTANDING   ....

YES / NO - GRASS   ....

YES / NO - WI-FI   ....

NOTES

....
....
....
....
....
....
....
....
....
....
....

MY 100 FAVOURITE GERMAN STELLPLATZ

DATE .... ARRIVAL TIME ....

AIRE NAME ....

ADDRESS 1 ....

ADDRESS 2 ....

REGION ....

WHAT3WORDS ///...

GPS ....

COST PER NIGHT € .... RECOMMEND – YES / NO

NO. OF NIGHTS HERE .... WEATHER ....

FACILITIES   **THINGS TO SEE / DO LOCALLY**

YES / NO - ELECTRICITY

YES / NO - FRESH WATER

YES / NO - BLACK WATER

YES / NO - GREY WATER

YES / NO - HARDSTANDING

YES / NO - GRASS

YES / NO - WI-FI

NOTES

MY 100 FAVOURITE
GERMAN STELLPLATZ

DATE .... ARRIVAL TIME ....

AIRE NAME ....

ADDRESS 1 ....

ADDRESS 2 ....

REGION ....

WHAT3WORDS ///...

GPS ....

COST PER NIGHT € .... RECOMMEND - YES / NO

NO. OF NIGHTS HERE .... WEATHER ....

FACILITIES

THINGS TO SEE / DO LOCALLY

YES / NO - ELECTRICITY

....

YES / NO - FRESH WATER

....

YES / NO - BLACK WATER

....

YES / NO - GREY WATER

....

YES / NO - HARDSTANDING

....

YES / NO - GRASS

....

YES / NO - WI-FI

....

NOTES

....
....
....
....
....
....
....
....
....
....
....
....

MY 100 FAVOURITE
GERMAN STELLPLATZ

DATE .... ARRIVAL TIME ....

AIRE NAME ....

ADDRESS 1 ....

ADDRESS 2 ....

REGION ....

WHAT3WORDS ///...

GPS ....

COST PER NIGHT € .... RECOMMEND - YES / NO

NO. OF NIGHTS HERE .... WEATHER ....

FACILITIES   THINGS TO SEE / DO LOCALLY

YES / NO - ELECTRICITY   ....

                           ....

YES / NO - FRESH WATER   ....

                           ....

YES / NO - BLACK WATER   ....

                           ....

YES / NO - GREY WATER   ....

                           ....

YES / NO - HARDSTANDING   ....

                           ....

YES / NO - GRASS   ....

                           ....

YES / NO - WI-FI   ....

NOTES

....
....
....
....
....
....
....
....
....
....
....

MY 100 FAVOURITE
GERMAN STELLPLATZ

DATE .... ARRIVAL TIME ....

AIRE NAME ....

ADDRESS 1 ....

ADDRESS 2 ....

REGION ....

WHAT3WORDS ///..

GPS ....

COST PER NIGHT € .... RECOMMEND - YES / NO

NO. OF NIGHTS HERE .... WEATHER ....

FACILITIES   THINGS TO SEE / DO LOCALLY

YES / NO - ELECTRICITY   ....

                                    ....
YES / NO - FRESH WATER   ....

                                    ....
YES / NO - BLACK WATER   ....

                                    ....
YES / NO - GREY WATER   ....

                                    ....
YES / NO - HARDSTANDING   ....

                                    ....
YES / NO - GRASS   ....

                                    ....
YES / NO - WI-FI   ....

                                    NOTES

....
....
....
....
....
....
....
....
....
....
....
....

MY 100 FAVOURITE
GERMAN STELLPLATZ

DATE .... ARRIVAL TIME ....

AIRE NAME ....

ADDRESS 1 ....

ADDRESS 2 ....

REGION ....

WHAT3WORDS ///..

GPS ....

COST PER NIGHT € .... RECOMMEND - YES / NO

NO. OF NIGHTS HERE .... WEATHER ....

FACILITIES   THINGS TO SEE / DO LOCALLY

YES / NO - ELECTRICITY   ....
                             ....
YES / NO - FRESH WATER   ....
                             ....
YES / NO - BLACK WATER   ....
                             ....
YES / NO - GREY WATER   ....
                             ....
YES / NO - HARDSTANDING   ....
                             ....
YES / NO - GRASS   ....
                             ....
YES / NO - WI-FI   ....

NOTES

....
....
....
....
....
....
....
....
....
....
....
....

MY 100 FAVOURITE
GERMAN STELLPLATZ

DATE .... ARRIVAL TIME ....

AIRE NAME ....

ADDRESS 1 ....

ADDRESS 2 ....

REGION ....

WHAT3WORDS ///..

GPS ....

COST PER NIGHT € .... RECOMMEND - YES / NO

NO. OF NIGHTS HERE .... WEATHER ....

FACILITIES   THINGS TO SEE / DO LOCALLY

YES / NO - ELECTRICITY

YES / NO - FRESH WATER

YES / NO - BLACK WATER

YES / NO - GREY WATER

YES / NO - HARDSTANDING

YES / NO - GRASS

YES / NO - WI-FI

NOTES

MY 100 FAVOURITE
GERMAN STELLPLATZ

DATE .... ARRIVAL TIME ....

AIRE NAME ....

ADDRESS 1 ....

ADDRESS 2 ....

REGION ....

WHAT3WORDS ///...

GPS ....

COST PER NIGHT € .... RECOMMEND – YES / NO

NO. OF NIGHTS HERE .... WEATHER ....

FACILITIES   THINGS TO SEE / DO LOCALLY

YES / NO – ELECTRICITY   ....

YES / NO – FRESH WATER   ....

YES / NO – BLACK WATER   ....

YES / NO – GREY WATER   ....

YES / NO – HARDSTANDING   ....

YES / NO – GRASS   ....

YES / NO – WI-FI   ....

NOTES

....
....
....
....
....
....
....
....
....
....
....
....

MY 100 FAVOURITE
GERMAN STELLPLATZ

DATE .... ARRIVAL TIME ....

AIRE NAME ....

ADDRESS 1 ....

ADDRESS 2 ....

REGION ....

WHAT3WORDS ///..

GPS ....

COST PER NIGHT € .... RECOMMEND - YES / NO

NO. OF NIGHTS HERE .... WEATHER ....

FACILITIES   THINGS TO SEE / DO LOCALLY

YES / NO - ELECTRICITY   ....
                              ....
YES / NO - FRESH WATER   ....
                              ....
YES / NO - BLACK WATER   ....
                              ....
YES / NO - GREY WATER   ....
                              ....
YES / NO - HARDSTANDING   ....
                              ....
YES / NO - GRASS   ....
                              ....
YES / NO - WI-FI   ....

NOTES

....
....
....
....
....
....
....
....
....
....

MY 100 FAVOURITE
GERMAN STELLPLATZ

DATE .... ARRIVAL TIME ....

AIRE NAME ....

ADDRESS 1 ....

ADDRESS 2 ....

REGION ....

WHAT3WORDS ///..

GPS ....

COST PER NIGHT € .... RECOMMEND - YES / NO

NO. OF NIGHTS HERE .... WEATHER ....

FACILITIES   THINGS TO SEE / DO LOCALLY

YES / NO - ELECTRICITY   ....
                                ....
YES / NO - FRESH WATER   ....
                                ....
YES / NO - BLACK WATER   ....
                                ....
YES / NO - GREY WATER   ....
                                ....
YES / NO - HARDSTANDING   ....
                                ....
YES / NO - GRASS   ....
                                ....
YES / NO - WI-FI   ....

NOTES

....
....
....
....
....
....
....
....
....
....
....

MY 100 FAVOURITE
GERMAN STELLPLATZ

DATE .... ARRIVAL TIME ....

AIRE NAME ....

ADDRESS 1 ....

ADDRESS 2 ....

REGION ....

WHAT3WORDS ///..

GPS ....

COST PER NIGHT € .... RECOMMEND - YES / NO

NO. OF NIGHTS HERE .... WEATHER ....

FACILITIES   THINGS TO SEE / DO LOCALLY

YES / NO - ELECTRICITY   ....

YES / NO - FRESH WATER   ....

YES / NO - BLACK WATER   ....

YES / NO - GREY WATER   ....

YES / NO - HARDSTANDING   ....

YES / NO - GRASS   ....

YES / NO - WI-FI   ....

NOTES

....
....
....
....
....
....
....
....
....
....
....
....

MY 100 FAVOURITE
GERMAN STELLPLATZ

DATE .... ARRIVAL TIME ....

AIRE NAME ....

ADDRESS 1 ....

ADDRESS 2 ....

REGION ....

WHAT3WORDS ///...

GPS ....

COST PER NIGHT € .... RECOMMEND - YES / NO

NO. OF NIGHTS HERE .... WEATHER ....

FACILITIES   THINGS TO SEE / DO LOCALLY

YES / NO - ELECTRICITY   ....
                                ....
YES / NO - FRESH WATER   ....
                                ....
YES / NO - BLACK WATER   ....
                                ....
YES / NO - GREY WATER   ....
                                ....
YES / NO - HARDSTANDING   ....
                                ....
YES / NO - GRASS   ....
                                ....
YES / NO - WI-FI   ....

NOTES

....
....
....
....
....
....
....
....
....
....
....

MY 100 FAVOURITE
GERMAN STELLPLATZ

DATE .... ARRIVAL TIME ....

AIRE NAME ....

ADDRESS 1 ....

ADDRESS 2 ....

REGION ....

WHAT3WORDS ///...

GPS ....

COST PER NIGHT € .... RECOMMEND - YES / NO

NO. OF NIGHTS HERE .... WEATHER ....

FACILITIES   THINGS TO SEE / DO LOCALLY

YES / NO - ELECTRICITY   ....

YES / NO - FRESH WATER   ....

YES / NO - BLACK WATER   ....

YES / NO - GREY WATER   ....

YES / NO - HARDSTANDING   ....

YES / NO - GRASS   ....

YES / NO - WI-FI   ....

NOTES

....

....

....

....

....

....

....

....

....

....

....

MY 100 FAVOURITE
GERMAN STELLPLATZ

DATE .... ARRIVAL TIME ....

AIRE NAME ....

ADDRESS 1 ....

ADDRESS 2 ....

REGION ....

WHAT3WORDS ///...

GPS ....

COST PER NIGHT € .... RECOMMEND - YES / NO

NO. OF NIGHTS HERE .... WEATHER ....

FACILITIES   THINGS TO SEE / DO LOCALLY

YES / NO - ELECTRICITY   ....
                                ....
YES / NO - FRESH WATER   ....
                                ....
YES / NO - BLACK WATER   ....
                                ....
YES / NO - GREY WATER   ....
                                ....
YES / NO - HARDSTANDING   ....
                                ....
YES / NO - GRASS   ....
                                ....
YES / NO - WI-FI   ....

NOTES

....
....
....
....
....
....
....
....
....
....

MY 100 FAVOURITE
GERMAN STELLPLATZ

DATE .... ARRIVAL TIME ....

AIRE NAME ....

ADDRESS 1 ....

ADDRESS 2 ....

REGION ....

WHAT3WORDS ///...

GPS ....

COST PER NIGHT € .... RECOMMEND - YES / NO

NO. OF NIGHTS HERE .... WEATHER ....

FACILITIES   THINGS TO SEE / DO LOCALLY

YES / NO - ELECTRICITY   ....

YES / NO - FRESH WATER   ....

YES / NO - BLACK WATER   ....

YES / NO - GREY WATER   ....

YES / NO - HARDSTANDING   ....

YES / NO - GRASS   ....

YES / NO - WI-FI   ....

NOTES

....
....
....
....
....
....
....
....
....
....

MY 100 FAVOURITE
GERMAN STELLPLATZ

DATE .... ARRIVAL TIME ....

AIRE NAME ....

ADDRESS 1 ....

ADDRESS 2 ....

REGION ....

WHAT3WORDS ///...

GPS ....

COST PER NIGHT € .... RECOMMEND - YES / NO

NO. OF NIGHTS HERE .... WEATHER ....

FACILITIES   THINGS TO SEE / DO LOCALLY

YES / NO - ELECTRICITY   ....
                              ....
YES / NO - FRESH WATER   ....
                              ....
YES / NO - BLACK WATER   ....
                              ....
YES / NO - GREY WATER   ....
                              ....
YES / NO - HARDSTANDING   ....
                              ....
YES / NO - GRASS   ....
                              ....
YES / NO - WI-FI   ....

NOTES

....
....
....
....
....
....
....
....
....
....
....
....

MY 100 FAVOURITE
GERMAN STELLPLATZ

DATE .... ARRIVAL TIME ....

AIRE NAME ....

ADDRESS 1 ....

ADDRESS 2 ....

REGION ....

WHAT3WORDS ///...

GPS ....

COST PER NIGHT € .... RECOMMEND - YES / NO

NO. OF NIGHTS HERE .... WEATHER ....

FACILITIES

THINGS TO SEE / DO LOCALLY

YES / NO - ELECTRICITY

YES / NO - FRESH WATER

YES / NO - BLACK WATER

YES / NO - GREY WATER

YES / NO - HARDSTANDING

YES / NO - GRASS

YES / NO - WI-FI

NOTES

....
....
....
....
....
....
....
....
....
....
....

MY 100 FAVOURITE
GERMAN STELLPLATZ

DATE .... ARRIVAL TIME ....

AIRE NAME ....

ADDRESS 1 ....

ADDRESS 2 ....

REGION ....

WHAT3WORDS ///..

GPS ....

COST PER NIGHT € .... RECOMMEND - YES / NO

NO. OF NIGHTS HERE .... WEATHER ....

FACILITIES   THINGS TO SEE / DO LOCALLY

YES / NO - ELECTRICITY   ....
                                ....
YES / NO - FRESH WATER   ....
                                ....
YES / NO - BLACK WATER   ....
                                ....
YES / NO - GREY WATER   ....
                                ....
YES / NO - HARDSTANDING   ....
                                ....
YES / NO - GRASS   ....
                                ....
YES / NO - WI-FI   ....

NOTES

....
....
....
....
....
....
....
....
....
....
....

MY 100 FAVOURITE GERMAN STELLPLATZ

DATE .... ARRIVAL TIME ....

AIRE NAME ....

ADDRESS 1 ....

ADDRESS 2 ....

REGION ....

WHAT3WORDS ///..

GPS ....

COST PER NIGHT € .... RECOMMEND - YES / NO

NO. OF NIGHTS HERE .... WEATHER ....

FACILITIES   THINGS TO SEE / DO LOCALLY

YES / NO - ELECTRICITY   ....

YES / NO - FRESH WATER   ....

YES / NO - BLACK WATER   ....

YES / NO - GREY WATER   ....

YES / NO - HARDSTANDING   ....

YES / NO - GRASS   ....

YES / NO - WI-FI   ....

NOTES

....

....

....

....

....

....

....

....

....

....

....

MY 100 FAVOURITE
GERMAN STELLPLATZ

DATE .... ARRIVAL TIME ....

AIRE NAME ....

ADDRESS 1 ....

ADDRESS 2 ....

REGION ....

WHAT3WORDS ///...

GPS ....

COST PER NIGHT € .... RECOMMEND - YES / NO

NO. OF NIGHTS HERE .... WEATHER ....

FACILITIES   THINGS TO SEE / DO LOCALLY

YES / NO - ELECTRICITY   ....

                                ....

YES / NO - FRESH WATER   ....

                                ....

YES / NO - BLACK WATER   ....

                                ....

YES / NO - GREY WATER   ....

                                ....

YES / NO - HARDSTANDING   ....

                                ....

YES / NO - GRASS   ....

                                ....

YES / NO - WI-FI   ....

                                ....

NOTES

....
....
....
....
....
....
....
....
....
....
....
....

MY 100 FAVOURITE
GERMAN STELLPLATZ

DATE .... ARRIVAL TIME ....

AIRE NAME ....

ADDRESS 1 ....

ADDRESS 2 ....

REGION ....

WHAT3WORDS ///...

GPS ....

COST PER NIGHT € .... RECOMMEND - YES / NO

NO. OF NIGHTS HERE .... WEATHER ....

FACILITIES

YES / NO - ELECTRICITY

YES / NO - FRESH WATER

YES / NO - BLACK WATER

YES / NO - GREY WATER

YES / NO - HARDSTANDING

YES / NO - GRASS

YES / NO - WI-FI

THINGS TO SEE / DO LOCALLY

....
....
....
....
....
....
....
....
....
....
....
....

NOTES

....
....
....
....
....
....
....
....
....
....
....
....

MY 100 FAVOURITE
GERMAN STELLPLATZ

DATE .... ARRIVAL TIME ....

AIRE NAME ....

ADDRESS 1 ....

ADDRESS 2 ....

REGION ....

WHAT3WORDS ///...

GPS ....

COST PER NIGHT € .... RECOMMEND - YES / NO

NO. OF NIGHTS HERE .... WEATHER ....

FACILITIES   THINGS TO SEE / DO LOCALLY

YES / NO - ELECTRICITY   ....
                            ....
YES / NO - FRESH WATER   ....
                            ....
YES / NO - BLACK WATER   ....
                            ....
YES / NO - GREY WATER   ....
                            ....
YES / NO - HARDSTANDING   ....
                            ....
YES / NO - GRASS   ....
                            ....
YES / NO - WI-FI   ....

NOTES

....
....
....
....
....
....
....
....
....
....
....

MY 100 FAVOURITE
GERMAN STELLPLATZ

DATE .... ARRIVAL TIME ....

AIRE NAME ....

ADDRESS 1 ....

ADDRESS 2 ....

REGION ....

WHAT3WORDS ///..

GPS ....

COST PER NIGHT € .... RECOMMEND - YES / NO

NO. OF NIGHTS HERE .... WEATHER ....

FACILITIES   THINGS TO SEE / DO LOCALLY

YES / NO - ELECTRICITY   ....

                              ....

YES / NO - FRESH WATER   ....

                              ....

YES / NO - BLACK WATER   ....

                              ....

YES / NO - GREY WATER   ....

                              ....

YES / NO - HARDSTANDING   ....

                              ....

YES / NO - GRASS   ....

                              ....

YES / NO - WI-FI   ....

NOTES

....
....
....
....
....
....
....
....
....
....
....

MY 100 FAVOURITE
GERMAN STELLPLATZ

DATE .... ARRIVAL TIME ....

AIRE NAME ....

ADDRESS 1 ....

ADDRESS 2 ....

REGION ....

WHAT3WORDS ///...

GPS ....

COST PER NIGHT € .... RECOMMEND - YES / NO

NO. OF NIGHTS HERE .... WEATHER ....

FACILITIES   THINGS TO SEE / DO LOCALLY

YES / NO - ELECTRICITY   ....
                            ....
YES / NO - FRESH WATER   ....
                            ....
YES / NO - BLACK WATER   ....
                            ....
YES / NO - GREY WATER   ....
                            ....
YES / NO - HARDSTANDING   ....
                            ....
YES / NO - GRASS   ....
                            ....
YES / NO - WI-FI   ....

NOTES

....
....
....
....
....
....
....
....
....
....

MY 100 FAVOURITE
GERMAN STELLPLATZ

DATE .... ARRIVAL TIME ....

AIRE NAME ....

ADDRESS 1 ....

ADDRESS 2 ....

REGION ....

WHAT3WORDS ///..

GPS ....

COST PER NIGHT € .... RECOMMEND - YES / NO

NO. OF NIGHTS HERE .... WEATHER ....

FACILITIES

THINGS TO SEE / DO LOCALLY

YES / NO - ELECTRICITY

YES / NO - FRESH WATER

YES / NO - BLACK WATER

YES / NO - GREY WATER

YES / NO - HARDSTANDING

YES / NO - GRASS

YES / NO - WI-FI

NOTES

MY 100 FAVOURITE
GERMAN STELLPLATZ

DATE .... ARRIVAL TIME ....

AIRE NAME ....

ADDRESS 1 ....

ADDRESS 2 ....

REGION ....

WHAT3WORDS ///..

GPS ....

COST PER NIGHT € .... RECOMMEND – YES / NO

NO. OF NIGHTS HERE .... WEATHER ....

FACILITIES   THINGS TO SEE / DO LOCALLY

YES / NO – ELECTRICITY   ....
                                ....
YES / NO – FRESH WATER   ....
                                ....
YES / NO – BLACK WATER   ....
                                ....
YES / NO – GREY WATER   ....
                                ....
YES / NO – HARDSTANDING   ....
                                ....
YES / NO – GRASS   ....
                                ....
YES / NO – WI-FI   ....

NOTES

....
....
....
....
....
....
....
....
....
....
....

MY 100 FAVOURITE
GERMAN STELLPLATZ

DATE .... ARRIVAL TIME ....

AIRE NAME ....

ADDRESS 1 ....

ADDRESS 2 ....

REGION ....

WHAT3WORDS ///..

GPS ....

COST PER NIGHT € .... RECOMMEND - YES / NO

NO. OF NIGHTS HERE .... WEATHER ....

FACILITIES   THINGS TO SEE / DO LOCALLY

YES / NO - ELECTRICITY

YES / NO - FRESH WATER

YES / NO - BLACK WATER

YES / NO - GREY WATER

YES / NO - HARDSTANDING

YES / NO - GRASS

YES / NO - WI-FI

NOTES

MY 100 FAVOURITE
GERMAN STELLPLATZ

DATE .... ARRIVAL TIME ....

AIRE NAME ....

ADDRESS 1 ....

ADDRESS 2 ....

REGION ....

WHAT3WORDS ///...

GPS ....

COST PER NIGHT € .... RECOMMEND - YES / NO

NO. OF NIGHTS HERE .... WEATHER ....

FACILITIES   THINGS TO SEE / DO LOCALLY

YES / NO - ELECTRICITY   ....
                                ....
YES / NO - FRESH WATER   ....
                                ....
YES / NO - BLACK WATER   ....
                                ....
YES / NO - GREY WATER   ....
                                ....
YES / NO - HARDSTANDING   ....
                                ....
YES / NO - GRASS   ....
                                ....
YES / NO - WI-FI   ....

NOTES

....
....
....
....
....
....
....
....
....
....
....

MY 100 FAVOURITE
GERMAN STELLPLATZ

DATE .... ARRIVAL TIME ....

AIRE NAME ....

ADDRESS 1 ....

ADDRESS 2 ....

REGION ....

WHAT3WORDS ///..

GPS ....

COST PER NIGHT € .... RECOMMEND - YES / NO

NO. OF NIGHTS HERE .... WEATHER ....

FACILITIES

THINGS TO SEE / DO LOCALLY

YES / NO - ELECTRICITY

YES / NO - FRESH WATER

YES / NO - BLACK WATER

YES / NO - GREY WATER

YES / NO - HARDSTANDING

YES / NO - GRASS

YES / NO - WI-FI

NOTES

MY 100 FAVOURITE
GERMAN STELLPLATZ

DATE .... ARRIVAL TIME ....

AIRE NAME ....

ADDRESS 1 ....

ADDRESS 2 ....

REGION ....

WHAT3WORDS ///...

GPS ....

COST PER NIGHT € .... RECOMMEND - YES / NO

NO. OF NIGHTS HERE .... WEATHER ....

FACILITIES   THINGS TO SEE / DO LOCALLY

YES / NO - ELECTRICITY   ....

YES / NO - FRESH WATER   ....

YES / NO - BLACK WATER   ....

YES / NO - GREY WATER   ....

YES / NO - HARDSTANDING   ....

YES / NO - GRASS   ....

YES / NO - WI-FI   ....

NOTES

....
....
....
....
....
....
....
....
....
....
....

MY 100 FAVOURITE
GERMAN STELLPLATZ

DATE .... ARRIVAL TIME ....

AIRE NAME ....

ADDRESS 1 ....

ADDRESS 2 ....

REGION ....

WHAT3WORDS ///...

GPS ....

COST PER NIGHT € .... RECOMMEND - YES / NO

NO. OF NIGHTS HERE .... WEATHER ....

FACILITIES   THINGS TO SEE / DO LOCALLY

YES / NO - ELECTRICITY   ....

YES / NO - FRESH WATER   ....

YES / NO - BLACK WATER   ....

YES / NO - GREY WATER   ....

YES / NO - HARDSTANDING   ....

YES / NO - GRASS   ....

YES / NO - WI-FI   ....

NOTES

....

....

....

....

....

....

....

....

....

....

....

MY 100 FAVOURITE
GERMAN STELLPLATZ

DATE .... ARRIVAL TIME ....

AIRE NAME ....

ADDRESS 1 ....

ADDRESS 2 ....

REGION ....

WHAT3WORDS ///..

GPS ....

COST PER NIGHT € .... RECOMMEND - YES / NO

NO. OF NIGHTS HERE .... WEATHER ....

FACILITIES   THINGS TO SEE / DO LOCALLY

YES / NO - ELECTRICITY

YES / NO - FRESH WATER

YES / NO - BLACK WATER

YES / NO - GREY WATER

YES / NO - HARDSTANDING

YES / NO - GRASS

YES / NO - WI-FI

NOTES

MY 100 FAVOURITE
GERMAN STELLPLATZ

DATE .... ARRIVAL TIME ....

AIRE NAME ....

ADDRESS 1 ....

ADDRESS 2 ....

REGION ....

WHAT3WORDS ///..

GPS ....

COST PER NIGHT € .... RECOMMEND – YES / NO

NO. OF NIGHTS HERE .... WEATHER ....

FACILITIES   THINGS TO SEE / DO LOCALLY

YES / NO – ELECTRICITY   ....

YES / NO – FRESH WATER   ....

YES / NO – BLACK WATER   ....

YES / NO – GREY WATER   ....

YES / NO – HARDSTANDING   ....

YES / NO – GRASS   ....

YES / NO – WI-FI   ....

NOTES

....

....

....

....

....

....

....

....

....

....

....

MY 100 FAVOURITE
GERMAN STELLPLATZ

DATE .... ARRIVAL TIME ....

AIRE NAME ....

ADDRESS 1 ....

ADDRESS 2 ....

REGION ....

WHAT3WORDS ///...

GPS ....

COST PER NIGHT € .... RECOMMEND - YES / NO

NO. OF NIGHTS HERE .... WEATHER ....

FACILITIES   THINGS TO SEE / DO LOCALLY

YES / NO - ELECTRICITY   ....

YES / NO - FRESH WATER   ....

YES / NO - BLACK WATER   ....

YES / NO - GREY WATER   ....

YES / NO - HARDSTANDING   ....

YES / NO - GRASS   ....

YES / NO - WI-FI   ....

NOTES

....
....
....
....
....
....
....
....
....
....
....

MY 100 FAVOURITE
GERMAN STELLPLATZ

DATE .... ARRIVAL TIME ....

AIRE NAME ....

ADDRESS 1 ....

ADDRESS 2 ....

REGION ....

WHAT3WORDS ///..

GPS ....

COST PER NIGHT € .... RECOMMEND - YES / NO

NO. OF NIGHTS HERE .... WEATHER ....

FACILITIES   THINGS TO SEE / DO LOCALLY

YES / NO - ELECTRICITY

YES / NO - FRESH WATER

YES / NO - BLACK WATER

YES / NO - GREY WATER

YES / NO - HARDSTANDING

YES / NO - GRASS

YES / NO - WI-FI

NOTES

MY 100 FAVOURITE
GERMAN STELLPLATZ

DATE .... ARRIVAL TIME ....

AIRE NAME ....

ADDRESS 1 ....

ADDRESS 2 ....

REGION ....

WHAT3WORDS ///...

GPS ....

COST PER NIGHT € .... RECOMMEND - YES / NO

NO. OF NIGHTS HERE .... WEATHER ....

FACILITIES   THINGS TO SEE / DO LOCALLY

YES / NO - ELECTRICITY   ....
                                ....
YES / NO - FRESH WATER   ....
                                ....
YES / NO - BLACK WATER   ....
                                ....
YES / NO - GREY WATER   ....
                                ....
YES / NO - HARDSTANDING   ....
                                ....
YES / NO - GRASS   ....
                                ....
YES / NO - WI-FI   ....

NOTES

....
....
....
....
....
....
....
....
....
....
....

MY 100 FAVOURITE
GERMAN STELLPLATZ

DATE .... ARRIVAL TIME ....

AIRE NAME ....

ADDRESS 1 ....

ADDRESS 2 ....

REGION ....

WHAT3WORDS ///..

GPS ....

COST PER NIGHT € .... RECOMMEND - YES / NO

NO. OF NIGHTS HERE .... WEATHER ....

FACILITIES   THINGS TO SEE / DO LOCALLY

YES / NO - ELECTRICITY   ....

YES / NO - FRESH WATER   ....

YES / NO - BLACK WATER   ....

YES / NO - GREY WATER   ....

YES / NO - HARDSTANDING   ....

YES / NO - GRASS   ....

YES / NO - WI-FI   ....

NOTES

....
....
....
....
....
....
....
....
....
....
....

MY 100 FAVOURITE
GERMAN STELLPLATZ

DATE .... ARRIVAL TIME ....

AIRE NAME ....

ADDRESS 1 ....

ADDRESS 2 ....

REGION ....

WHAT3WORDS ///..

GPS ....

COST PER NIGHT € .... RECOMMEND - YES / NO

NO. OF NIGHTS HERE .... WEATHER ....

FACILITIES   THINGS TO SEE / DO LOCALLY

YES / NO - ELECTRICITY   ....
                                ....
YES / NO - FRESH WATER   ....
                                ....
YES / NO - BLACK WATER   ....
                                ....
YES / NO - GREY WATER   ....
                                ....
YES / NO - HARDSTANDING   ....
                                ....
YES / NO - GRASS   ....
                                ....
YES / NO - WI-FI   ....

NOTES

....
....
....
....
....
....
....
....
....
....
....

MY 100 FAVOURITE
GERMAN STELLPLATZ

DATE .... ARRIVAL TIME ....

AIRE NAME ....

ADDRESS 1 ....

ADDRESS 2 ....

REGION ....

WHAT3WORDS ///..

GPS ....

COST PER NIGHT € .... RECOMMEND - YES / NO

NO. OF NIGHTS HERE .... WEATHER ....

FACILITIES   THINGS TO SEE / DO LOCALLY

YES / NO - ELECTRICITY   ....
                                ....
YES / NO - FRESH WATER   ....
                                ....
YES / NO - BLACK WATER   ....
                                ....
YES / NO - GREY WATER   ....
                                ....
YES / NO - HARDSTANDING   ....
                                ....
YES / NO - GRASS   ....
                                ....
YES / NO - WI-FI   ....

NOTES

....
....
....
....
....
....
....
....
....
....
....

MY 100 FAVOURITE
GERMAN STELLPLATZ

DATE .... ARRIVAL TIME ....

AIRE NAME ....

ADDRESS 1 ....

ADDRESS 2 ....

REGION ....

WHAT3WORDS ///..

GPS ....

COST PER NIGHT € .... RECOMMEND - YES / NO

NO. OF NIGHTS HERE .... WEATHER ....

FACILITIES   THINGS TO SEE / DO LOCALLY

YES / NO - ELECTRICITY   ....

YES / NO - FRESH WATER   ....

YES / NO - BLACK WATER   ....

YES / NO - GREY WATER   ....

YES / NO - HARDSTANDING   ....

YES / NO - GRASS   ....

YES / NO - WI-FI   ....

NOTES

....
....
....
....
....
....
....
....
....
....
....

MY 100 FAVOURITE
GERMAN STELLPLATZ

DATE .... ARRIVAL TIME ....

AIRE NAME ....

ADDRESS 1 ....

ADDRESS 2 ....

REGION ....

WHAT3WORDS ///..

GPS ....

COST PER NIGHT € .... RECOMMEND - YES / NO

NO. OF NIGHTS HERE .... WEATHER ....

FACILITIES   THINGS TO SEE / DO LOCALLY

YES / NO - ELECTRICITY   ....

YES / NO - FRESH WATER   ....

YES / NO - BLACK WATER   ....

YES / NO - GREY WATER   ....

YES / NO - HARDSTANDING   ....

YES / NO - GRASS   ....

YES / NO - WI-FI   ....

NOTES

....
....
....
....
....
....
....
....
....
....
....

MY 100 FAVOURITE
GERMAN STELLPLATZ

DATE .... ARRIVAL TIME ....

AIRE NAME ....

ADDRESS 1 ....

ADDRESS 2 ....

REGION ....

WHAT3WORDS ///...

GPS ....

COST PER NIGHT € .... RECOMMEND - YES / NO

NO. OF NIGHTS HERE .... WEATHER ....

FACILITIES   THINGS TO SEE / DO LOCALLY

YES / NO - ELECTRICITY   ....
                                  ....
YES / NO - FRESH WATER   ....
                                  ....
YES / NO - BLACK WATER   ....
                                  ....
YES / NO - GREY WATER   ....
                                  ....
YES / NO - HARDSTANDING   ....
                                  ....
YES / NO - GRASS   ....
                                  ....
YES / NO - WI-FI   ....

NOTES

....
....
....
....
....
....
....
....
....
....
....

MY 100 FAVOURITE
GERMAN STELLPLATZ

DATE .... ARRIVAL TIME ....

AIRE NAME ....

ADDRESS 1 ....

ADDRESS 2 ....

REGION ....

WHAT3WORDS ///...

GPS ....

COST PER NIGHT € .... RECOMMEND - YES / NO

NO. OF NIGHTS HERE .... WEATHER ....

FACILITIES   THINGS TO SEE / DO LOCALLY

YES / NO - ELECTRICITY   ....

YES / NO - FRESH WATER   ....

YES / NO - BLACK WATER   ....

YES / NO - GREY WATER   ....

YES / NO - HARDSTANDING   ....

YES / NO - GRASS   ....

YES / NO - WI-FI   ....

NOTES

....
....
....
....
....
....
....
....
....
....

MY 100 FAVOURITE
GERMAN STELLPLATZ

DATE .... ARRIVAL TIME ....

AIRE NAME ....

ADDRESS 1 ....

ADDRESS 2 ....

REGION ....

WHAT3WORDS ///..

GPS ....

COST PER NIGHT € .... RECOMMEND – YES / NO

NO. OF NIGHTS HERE .... WEATHER ....

FACILITIES   THINGS TO SEE / DO LOCALLY

YES / NO - ELECTRICITY   ....

YES / NO - FRESH WATER   ....

YES / NO - BLACK WATER   ....

YES / NO - GREY WATER   ....

YES / NO - HARDSTANDING   ....

YES / NO - GRASS   ....

YES / NO - WI-FI   ....

NOTES

....
....
....
....
....
....
....
....
....
....
....

MY 100 FAVOURITE
GERMAN STELLPLATZ

DATE .... ARRIVAL TIME ....

AIRE NAME ....

ADDRESS 1 ....

ADDRESS 2 ....

REGION ....

WHAT3WORDS ///..

GPS ....

COST PER NIGHT € .... RECOMMEND - YES / NO

NO. OF NIGHTS HERE .... WEATHER ....

FACILITIES   THINGS TO SEE / DO LOCALLY

YES / NO - ELECTRICITY   ....

YES / NO - FRESH WATER   ....

YES / NO - BLACK WATER   ....

YES / NO - GREY WATER   ....

YES / NO - HARDSTANDING   ....

YES / NO - GRASS   ....

YES / NO - WI-FI   ....

NOTES

....
....
....
....
....
....
....
....
....
....

MY 100 FAVOURITE
GERMAN STELLPLATZ

DATE .... ARRIVAL TIME ....

AIRE NAME ....

ADDRESS 1 ....

ADDRESS 2 ....

REGION ....

WHAT3WORDS ///..

GPS ....

COST PER NIGHT € .... RECOMMEND – YES / NO

NO. OF NIGHTS HERE .... WEATHER ....

FACILITIES   THINGS TO SEE / DO LOCALLY

YES / NO – ELECTRICITY   ....

YES / NO – FRESH WATER   ....

YES / NO – BLACK WATER   ....

YES / NO – GREY WATER   ....

YES / NO – HARDSTANDING   ....

YES / NO – GRASS   ....

YES / NO – WI-FI   ....

NOTES

....
....
....
....
....
....
....
....
....
....
....

MY 100 FAVOURITE
GERMAN STELLPLATZ

DATE .... ARRIVAL TIME ....

AIRE NAME ....

ADDRESS 1 ....

ADDRESS 2 ....

REGION ....

WHAT3WORDS ///..

GPS ....

COST PER NIGHT € .... RECOMMEND - YES / NO

NO. OF NIGHTS HERE .... WEATHER ....

FACILITIES   THINGS TO SEE / DO LOCALLY

YES / NO - ELECTRICITY   ....

YES / NO - FRESH WATER   ....

YES / NO - BLACK WATER   ....

YES / NO - GREY WATER   ....

YES / NO - HARDSTANDING   ....

YES / NO - GRASS   ....

YES / NO - WI-FI   ....

NOTES

....
....
....
....
....
....
....
....
....
....
....

MY 100 FAVOURITE
GERMAN STELLPLATZ

DATE .... ARRIVAL TIME ....

AIRE NAME ....

ADDRESS 1 ....

ADDRESS 2 ....

REGION ....

WHAT3WORDS ///..

GPS ....

COST PER NIGHT € .... RECOMMEND - YES / NO

NO. OF NIGHTS HERE .... WEATHER ....

FACILITIES   THINGS TO SEE / DO LOCALLY

YES / NO - ELECTRICITY   ....

YES / NO - FRESH WATER   ....

YES / NO - BLACK WATER   ....

YES / NO - GREY WATER   ....

YES / NO - HARDSTANDING   ....

YES / NO - GRASS   ....

YES / NO - WI-FI   ....

NOTES

....
....
....
....
....
....
....
....
....
....
....

MY 100 FAVOURITE
GERMAN STELLPLATZ

DATE .... ARRIVAL TIME ....

AIRE NAME ....

ADDRESS 1 ....

ADDRESS 2 ....

REGION ....

WHAT3WORDS ///..

GPS ....

COST PER NIGHT € .... RECOMMEND - YES / NO

NO. OF NIGHTS HERE .... WEATHER ....

FACILITIES   THINGS TO SEE / DO LOCALLY

YES / NO - ELECTRICITY   ....

YES / NO - FRESH WATER   ....

YES / NO - BLACK WATER   ....

YES / NO - GREY WATER   ....

YES / NO - HARDSTANDING   ....

YES / NO - GRASS   ....

YES / NO - WI-FI   ....

NOTES

....
....
....
....
....
....
....
....
....
....
....

MY 100 FAVOURITE
GERMAN STELLPLATZ

DATE .... ARRIVAL TIME ....

AIRE NAME ....

ADDRESS 1 ....

ADDRESS 2 ....

REGION ....

WHAT3WORDS ///..

GPS ....

COST PER NIGHT € .... RECOMMEND – YES / NO

NO. OF NIGHTS HERE .... WEATHER ....

FACILITIES   THINGS TO SEE / DO LOCALLY

YES / NO - ELECTRICITY   ....
                              ....
YES / NO - FRESH WATER   ....
                              ....
YES / NO - BLACK WATER   ....
                              ....
YES / NO - GREY WATER   ....
                              ....
YES / NO - HARDSTANDING   ....
                              ....
YES / NO - GRASS   ....
                              ....
YES / NO - WI-FI   ....

NOTES

....
....
....
....
....
....
....
....
....
....
....

MY 100 FAVOURITE GERMAN STELLPLATZ

DATE .... ARRIVAL TIME ....

AIRE NAME ....

ADDRESS 1 ....

ADDRESS 2 ....

REGION ....

WHAT3WORDS ///...

GPS ....

COST PER NIGHT € .... RECOMMEND - YES / NO

NO. OF NIGHTS HERE .... WEATHER ....

FACILITIES

YES / NO - ELECTRICITY

YES / NO - FRESH WATER

YES / NO - BLACK WATER

YES / NO - GREY WATER

YES / NO - HARDSTANDING

YES / NO - GRASS

YES / NO - WI-FI

THINGS TO SEE / DO LOCALLY

....
....
....
....
....
....
....
....
....
....

NOTES

....
....
....
....
....
....
....
....
....
....
....

MY 100 FAVOURITE
GERMAN STELLPLATZ

DATE .... ARRIVAL TIME ....

AIRE NAME ....

ADDRESS 1 ....

ADDRESS 2 ....

REGION ....

WHAT3WORDS ///...

GPS ....

COST PER NIGHT € .... RECOMMEND - YES / NO

NO. OF NIGHTS HERE .... WEATHER ....

FACILITIES   THINGS TO SEE / DO LOCALLY

YES / NO - ELECTRICITY   ....
                                ....
YES / NO - FRESH WATER   ....
                                ....
YES / NO - BLACK WATER   ....
                                ....
YES / NO - GREY WATER   ....
                                ....
YES / NO - HARDSTANDING   ....
                                ....
YES / NO - GRASS   ....
                                ....
YES / NO - WI-FI   ....

NOTES

....
....
....
....
....
....
....
....
....
....
....

MY 100 FAVOURITE
GERMAN STELLPLATZ

DATE .... ARRIVAL TIME ....

AIRE NAME ....

ADDRESS 1 ....

ADDRESS 2 ....

REGION ....

WHAT3WORDS ///..

GPS ....

COST PER NIGHT € .... RECOMMEND - YES / NO

NO. OF NIGHTS HERE .... WEATHER ....

FACILITIES

THINGS TO SEE / DO LOCALLY

YES / NO - ELECTRICITY

YES / NO - FRESH WATER

YES / NO - BLACK WATER

YES / NO - GREY WATER

YES / NO - HARDSTANDING

YES / NO - GRASS

YES / NO - WI-FI

NOTES

MY 100 FAVOURITE
GERMAN STELLPLATZ

DATE .... ARRIVAL TIME ....

AIRE NAME ....

ADDRESS 1 ....

ADDRESS 2 ....

REGION ....

WHAT3WORDS ///...

GPS ....

COST PER NIGHT € .... RECOMMEND - YES / NO

NO. OF NIGHTS HERE .... WEATHER ....

FACILITIES   THINGS TO SEE / DO LOCALLY

YES / NO - ELECTRICITY   ....
                                ....
YES / NO - FRESH WATER   ....
                                ....
YES / NO - BLACK WATER   ....
                                ....
YES / NO - GREY WATER   ....
                                ....
YES / NO - HARDSTANDING   ....
                                ....
YES / NO - GRASS   ....
                                ....
YES / NO - WI-FI   ....

NOTES

....
....
....
....
....
....
....
....
....
....
....
....

MY 100 FAVOURITE
GERMAN STELLPLATZ

DATE .... ARRIVAL TIME ....

AIRE NAME ....

ADDRESS 1 ....

ADDRESS 2 ....

REGION ....

WHAT3WORDS ///..

GPS ....

COST PER NIGHT € .... RECOMMEND - YES / NO

NO. OF NIGHTS HERE .... WEATHER ....

FACILITIES   **THINGS TO SEE / DO LOCALLY**

YES / NO - ELECTRICITY   ....

YES / NO - FRESH WATER   ....

YES / NO - BLACK WATER   ....

YES / NO - GREY WATER   ....

YES / NO - HARDSTANDING   ....

YES / NO - GRASS   ....

YES / NO - WI-FI   ....

NOTES

....
....
....
....
....
....
....
....
....
....

MY 100 FAVOURITE
GERMAN STELLPLATZ

DATE .... ARRIVAL TIME ....

AIRE NAME ....

ADDRESS 1 ....

ADDRESS 2 ....

REGION ....

WHAT3WORDS ///...

GPS ....

COST PER NIGHT € .... RECOMMEND - YES / NO

NO. OF NIGHTS HERE .... WEATHER ....

FACILITIES   THINGS TO SEE / DO LOCALLY

YES / NO - ELECTRICITY   ....
                              ....
YES / NO - FRESH WATER   ....
                              ....
YES / NO - BLACK WATER   ....
                              ....
YES / NO - GREY WATER   ....
                              ....
YES / NO - HARDSTANDING   ....
                              ....
YES / NO - GRASS   ....
                              ....
YES / NO - WI-FI   ....

NOTES

....
....
....
....
....
....
....
....
....
....
....

MY 100 FAVOURITE
GERMAN STELLPLATZ

DATE .... ARRIVAL TIME ....

AIRE NAME ....

ADDRESS 1 ....

ADDRESS 2 ....

REGION ....

WHAT3WORDS ///..

GPS ....

COST PER NIGHT € .... RECOMMEND – YES / NO

NO. OF NIGHTS HERE .... WEATHER ....

FACILITIES   THINGS TO SEE / DO LOCALLY

YES / NO – ELECTRICITY   ....
                             ....
YES / NO – FRESH WATER   ....
                             ....
YES / NO – BLACK WATER   ....
                             ....
YES / NO – GREY WATER   ....
                             ....
YES / NO – HARDSTANDING   ....
                             ....
YES / NO – GRASS   ....
                             ....
YES / NO – WI-FI   ....

NOTES

....
....
....
....
....
....
....
....
....
....
....

MY 100 FAVOURITE
GERMAN STELLPLATZ

DATE .... ARRIVAL TIME ....

AIRE NAME ....

ADDRESS 1 ....

ADDRESS 2 ....

REGION ....

WHAT3WORDS ///...

GPS ....

COST PER NIGHT € .... RECOMMEND - YES / NO

NO. OF NIGHTS HERE .... WEATHER ....

FACILITIES   THINGS TO SEE / DO LOCALLY

YES / NO - ELECTRICITY   ....

YES / NO - FRESH WATER   ....

YES / NO - BLACK WATER   ....

YES / NO - GREY WATER   ....

YES / NO - HARDSTANDING   ....

YES / NO - GRASS   ....

YES / NO - WI-FI   ....

NOTES

....
....
....
....
....
....
....
....
....
....
....
....

MY 100 FAVOURITE
GERMAN STELLPLATZ

DATE .... ARRIVAL TIME ....

AIRE NAME ....

ADDRESS 1 ....

ADDRESS 2 ....

REGION ....

WHAT3WORDS ///...

GPS ....

COST PER NIGHT € .... RECOMMEND - YES / NO

NO. OF NIGHTS HERE .... WEATHER ....

FACILITIES

YES / NO - ELECTRICITY

YES / NO - FRESH WATER

YES / NO - BLACK WATER

YES / NO - GREY WATER

YES / NO - HARDSTANDING

YES / NO - GRASS

YES / NO - WI-FI

THINGS TO SEE / DO LOCALLY

....
....
....
....
....
....
....
....
....
....

NOTES

....
....
....
....
....
....
....
....
....
....
....
....

MY 100 FAVOURITE
GERMAN STELLPLATZ

DATE .... ARRIVAL TIME ....

AIRE NAME ....

ADDRESS 1 ....

ADDRESS 2 ....

REGION ....

WHAT3WORDS ///..

GPS ....

COST PER NIGHT € .... RECOMMEND - YES / NO

NO. OF NIGHTS HERE .... WEATHER ....

FACILITIES   THINGS TO SEE / DO LOCALLY

YES / NO - ELECTRICITY   ....
                                    ....
YES / NO - FRESH WATER   ....
                                    ....
YES / NO - BLACK WATER   ....
                                    ....
YES / NO - GREY WATER   ....
                                    ....
YES / NO - HARDSTANDING   ....
                                    ....
YES / NO - GRASS   ....
                                    ....
YES / NO - WI-FI   ....

NOTES

....
....
....
....
....
....
....
....
....
....
....

MY 100 FAVOURITE
GERMAN STELLPLATZ

DATE .... ARRIVAL TIME ....

AIRE NAME ....

ADDRESS 1 ....

ADDRESS 2 ....

REGION ....

WHAT3WORDS ///..

GPS ....

COST PER NIGHT € .... RECOMMEND – YES / NO

NO. OF NIGHTS HERE .... WEATHER ....

FACILITIES   THINGS TO SEE / DO LOCALLY

YES / NO – ELECTRICITY   ....

YES / NO – FRESH WATER   ....

YES / NO – BLACK WATER   ....

YES / NO – GREY WATER   ....

YES / NO – HARDSTANDING   ....

YES / NO – GRASS   ....

YES / NO – WI-FI   ....

NOTES

....
....
....
....
....
....
....
....
....
....

MY 100 FAVOURITE
GERMAN STELLPLATZ

DATE .... ARRIVAL TIME ....

AIRE NAME ....

ADDRESS 1 ....

ADDRESS 2 ....

REGION ....

WHAT3WORDS ///..

GPS ....

COST PER NIGHT € .... RECOMMEND – YES / NO

NO. OF NIGHTS HERE .... WEATHER ....

FACILITIES   THINGS TO SEE / DO LOCALLY

YES / NO – ELECTRICITY

YES / NO – FRESH WATER

YES / NO – BLACK WATER

YES / NO – GREY WATER

YES / NO – HARDSTANDING

YES / NO – GRASS

YES / NO – WI-FI

NOTES

MY 100 FAVOURITE
GERMAN STELLPLATZ

DATE .... ARRIVAL TIME ....

AIRE NAME ....

ADDRESS 1 ....

ADDRESS 2 ....

REGION ....

WHAT3WORDS ///..

GPS ....

COST PER NIGHT € .... RECOMMEND – YES / NO

NO. OF NIGHTS HERE .... WEATHER ....

FACILITIES   **THINGS TO SEE / DO LOCALLY**

YES / NO - ELECTRICITY   ....

YES / NO - FRESH WATER   ....

YES / NO - BLACK WATER   ....

YES / NO - GREY WATER   ....

YES / NO - HARDSTANDING   ....

YES / NO - GRASS   ....

YES / NO - WI-FI   ....

NOTES

....
....
....
....
....
....
....
....
....
....
....

MY 100 FAVOURITE
GERMAN STELLPLATZ

DATE .... ARRIVAL TIME ....

AIRE NAME ....

ADDRESS 1 ....

ADDRESS 2 ....

REGION ....

WHAT3WORDS ///..

GPS ....

COST PER NIGHT € .... RECOMMEND – YES / NO

NO. OF NIGHTS HERE .... WEATHER ....

FACILITIES   THINGS TO SEE / DO LOCALLY

YES / NO – ELECTRICITY   ....

YES / NO – FRESH WATER   ....

YES / NO – BLACK WATER   ....

YES / NO – GREY WATER   ....

YES / NO – HARDSTANDING   ....

YES / NO – GRASS   ....

YES / NO – WI-FI   ....

NOTES

....
....
....
....
....
....
....
....
....
....
....

MY 100 FAVOURITE GERMAN STELLPLATZ

DATE .... ARRIVAL TIME ....

AIRE NAME ....

ADDRESS 1 ....

ADDRESS 2 ....

REGION ....

WHAT3WORDS ///..

GPS ....

COST PER NIGHT € .... RECOMMEND - YES / NO

NO. OF NIGHTS HERE .... WEATHER ....

FACILITIES

THINGS TO SEE / DO LOCALLY

YES / NO - ELECTRICITY

YES / NO - FRESH WATER

YES / NO - BLACK WATER

YES / NO - GREY WATER

YES / NO - HARDSTANDING

YES / NO - GRASS

YES / NO - WI-FI

NOTES

MY 100 FAVOURITE
GERMAN STELLPLATZ

DATE .... ARRIVAL TIME ....

AIRE NAME ....

ADDRESS 1 ....

ADDRESS 2 ....

REGION ....

WHAT3WORDS ///..

GPS ....

COST PER NIGHT € .... RECOMMEND - YES / NO

NO. OF NIGHTS HERE .... WEATHER ....

FACILITIES   THINGS TO SEE / DO LOCALLY

YES / NO - ELECTRICITY   ....
                              ....
YES / NO - FRESH WATER   ....
                              ....
YES / NO - BLACK WATER   ....
                              ....
YES / NO - GREY WATER   ....
                              ....
YES / NO - HARDSTANDING   ....
                              ....
YES / NO - GRASS   ....
                              ....
YES / NO - WI-FI   ....

NOTES

....
....
....
....
....
....
....
....
....
....
....
....

MY 100 FAVOURITE
GERMAN STELLPLATZ

DATE .... ARRIVAL TIME ....

AIRE NAME ....

ADDRESS 1 ....

ADDRESS 2 ....

REGION ....

WHAT3WORDS ///..

GPS ....

COST PER NIGHT € .... RECOMMEND - YES / NO

NO. OF NIGHTS HERE .... WEATHER ....

FACILITIES   **THINGS TO SEE / DO LOCALLY**

YES / NO - ELECTRICITY   ....

YES / NO - FRESH WATER   ....

YES / NO - BLACK WATER   ....

YES / NO - GREY WATER   ....

YES / NO - HARDSTANDING   ....

YES / NO - GRASS   ....

YES / NO - WI-FI   ....

NOTES

....
....
....
....
....
....
....
....
....
....

MY 100 FAVOURITE
GERMAN STELLPLATZ

DATE .... ARRIVAL TIME ....

AIRE NAME ....

ADDRESS 1 ....

ADDRESS 2 ....

REGION ....

WHAT3WORDS ///...

GPS ....

COST PER NIGHT € .... RECOMMEND – YES / NO

NO. OF NIGHTS HERE .... WEATHER ....

FACILITIES   THINGS TO SEE / DO LOCALLY

YES / NO – ELECTRICITY   ....
                              ....
YES / NO – FRESH WATER   ....
                              ....
YES / NO – BLACK WATER   ....
                              ....
YES / NO – GREY WATER   ....
                              ....
YES / NO – HARDSTANDING   ....
                              ....
YES / NO – GRASS   ....
                              ....
YES / NO – WI-FI   ....

NOTES

....
....
....
....
....
....
....
....
....
....
....
....

MY 100 FAVOURITE
GERMAN STELLPLATZ

DATE .... ARRIVAL TIME ....

AIRE NAME ....

ADDRESS 1 ....

ADDRESS 2 ....

REGION ....

WHAT3WORDS ///...

GPS ....

COST PER NIGHT € .... RECOMMEND - YES / NO

NO. OF NIGHTS HERE .... WEATHER ....

FACILITIES

THINGS TO SEE / DO LOCALLY

YES / NO - ELECTRICITY

....

....

YES / NO - FRESH WATER

....

....

YES / NO - BLACK WATER

....

....

YES / NO - GREY WATER

....

....

YES / NO - HARDSTANDING

....

....

YES / NO - GRASS

....

....

YES / NO - WI-FI

....

NOTES

....
....
....
....
....
....
....
....
....
....
....
....

MY 100 FAVOURITE
GERMAN STELLPLATZ

DATE .... ARRIVAL TIME ....

AIRE NAME ....

ADDRESS 1 ....

ADDRESS 2 ....

REGION ....

WHAT3WORDS ///...

GPS ....

COST PER NIGHT € .... RECOMMEND - YES / NO

NO. OF NIGHTS HERE .... WEATHER ....

FACILITIES   THINGS TO SEE / DO LOCALLY

YES / NO - ELECTRICITY   ....
                             ....
YES / NO - FRESH WATER   ....
                             ....
YES / NO - BLACK WATER   ....
                             ....
YES / NO - GREY WATER   ....
                             ....
YES / NO - HARDSTANDING   ....
                             ....
YES / NO - GRASS   ....
                             ....
YES / NO - WI-FI   ....

NOTES

....
....
....
....
....
....
....
....
....
....
....

MY 100 FAVOURITE
GERMAN STELLPLATZ

DATE .... ARRIVAL TIME ....

AIRE NAME ....

ADDRESS 1 ....

ADDRESS 2 ....

REGION ....

WHAT3WORDS ///...

GPS ....

COST PER NIGHT € .... RECOMMEND - YES / NO

NO. OF NIGHTS HERE .... WEATHER ....

FACILITIES   THINGS TO SEE / DO LOCALLY

YES / NO - ELECTRICITY   ....
                              ....
YES / NO - FRESH WATER   ....
                              ....
YES / NO - BLACK WATER   ....
                              ....
YES / NO - GREY WATER   ....
                              ....
YES / NO - HARDSTANDING   ....
                              ....
YES / NO - GRASS   ....
                              ....
YES / NO - WI-FI   ....

NOTES

....
....
....
....
....
....
....
....
....
....
....
....

MY 100 FAVOURITE GERMAN STELLPLATZ

DATE .... ARRIVAL TIME ....

AIRE NAME ....

ADDRESS 1 ....

ADDRESS 2 ....

REGION ....

WHAT3WORDS ///...

GPS ....

COST PER NIGHT € .... RECOMMEND - YES / NO

NO. OF NIGHTS HERE .... WEATHER ....

FACILITIES   THINGS TO SEE / DO LOCALLY

YES / NO - ELECTRICITY   ....
                                ....
YES / NO - FRESH WATER   ....
                                ....
YES / NO - BLACK WATER   ....
                                ....
YES / NO - GREY WATER   ....
                                ....
YES / NO - HARDSTANDING   ....
                                ....
YES / NO - GRASS   ....
                                ....
YES / NO - WI-FI   ....

NOTES

....
....
....
....
....
....
....
....
....
....
....
....

MY 100 FAVOURITE
GERMAN STELLPLATZ

DATE .... ARRIVAL TIME ....

AIRE NAME ....

ADDRESS 1 ....

ADDRESS 2 ....

REGION ....

WHAT3WORDS ///...

GPS ....

COST PER NIGHT € .... RECOMMEND - YES / NO

NO. OF NIGHTS HERE .... WEATHER ....

FACILITIES   THINGS TO SEE / DO LOCALLY

YES / NO - ELECTRICITY   ....

YES / NO - FRESH WATER   ....

YES / NO - BLACK WATER   ....

YES / NO - GREY WATER   ....

YES / NO - HARDSTANDING   ....

YES / NO - GRASS   ....

YES / NO - WI-FI   ....

NOTES

....
....
....
....
....
....
....
....
....
....

MY 100 FAVOURITE
GERMAN STELLPLATZ

DATE .... ARRIVAL TIME ....

AIRE NAME ....

ADDRESS 1 ....

ADDRESS 2 ....

REGION ....

WHAT3WORDS ///..

GPS ....

COST PER NIGHT € .... RECOMMEND - YES / NO

NO. OF NIGHTS HERE .... WEATHER ....

FACILITIES   THINGS TO SEE / DO LOCALLY

YES / NO - ELECTRICITY   ....
                                ....
YES / NO - FRESH WATER   ....
                                ....
YES / NO - BLACK WATER   ....
                                ....
YES / NO - GREY WATER   ....
                                ....
YES / NO - HARDSTANDING   ....
                                ....
YES / NO - GRASS   ....
                                ....
YES / NO - WI-FI   ....

NOTES

....
....
....
....
....
....
....
....
....
....
....
....

MY 100 FAVOURITE
GERMAN STELLPLATZ

DATE .... ARRIVAL TIME ....

AIRE NAME ....

ADDRESS 1 ....

ADDRESS 2 ....

REGION ....

WHAT3WORDS ///..

GPS ....

COST PER NIGHT € .... RECOMMEND - YES / NO

NO. OF NIGHTS HERE .... WEATHER ....

FACILITIES   THINGS TO SEE / DO LOCALLY

YES / NO - ELECTRICITY   ....

YES / NO - FRESH WATER   ....

YES / NO - BLACK WATER   ....

YES / NO - GREY WATER   ....

YES / NO - HARDSTANDING   ....

YES / NO - GRASS   ....

YES / NO - WI-FI   ....

NOTES

....
....
....
....
....
....
....
....
....
....
....

MY 100 FAVOURITE
GERMAN STELLPLATZ

DATE .... ARRIVAL TIME ....

AIRE NAME ....

ADDRESS 1 ....

ADDRESS 2 ....

REGION ....

WHAT3WORDS ///...

GPS ....

COST PER NIGHT € .... RECOMMEND - YES / NO

NO. OF NIGHTS HERE .... WEATHER ....

FACILITIES   THINGS TO SEE / DO LOCALLY

YES / NO - ELECTRICITY   ....
                              ....
YES / NO - FRESH WATER   ....
                              ....
YES / NO - BLACK WATER   ....
                              ....
YES / NO - GREY WATER   ....
                              ....
YES / NO - HARDSTANDING   ....
                              ....
YES / NO - GRASS   ....
                              ....
YES / NO - WI-FI   ....

NOTES

....
....
....
....
....
....
....
....
....
....
....

MY 100 FAVOURITE
GERMAN STELLPLATZ

DATE .... ARRIVAL TIME ....

AIRE NAME ....

ADDRESS 1 ....

ADDRESS 2 ....

REGION ....

WHAT3WORDS ///..

GPS ....

COST PER NIGHT € .... RECOMMEND - YES / NO

NO. OF NIGHTS HERE .... WEATHER ....

FACILITIES   THINGS TO SEE / DO LOCALLY

YES / NO - ELECTRICITY   ....
                            ....
YES / NO - FRESH WATER   ....
                            ....
YES / NO - BLACK WATER   ....
                            ....
YES / NO - GREY WATER   ....
                            ....
YES / NO - HARDSTANDING   ....
                            ....
YES / NO - GRASS   ....
                            ....
YES / NO - WI-FI   ....

                         NOTES

....
....
....
....
....
....
....
....
....
....
....

MY 100 FAVOURITE
GERMAN STELLPLATZ

DATE .... ARRIVAL TIME ....

AIRE NAME ....

ADDRESS 1 ....

ADDRESS 2 ....

REGION ....

WHAT3WORDS ///...

GPS ....

COST PER NIGHT € .... RECOMMEND - YES / NO

NO. OF NIGHTS HERE .... WEATHER ....

FACILITIES   THINGS TO SEE / DO LOCALLY

YES / NO - ELECTRICITY   ....

YES / NO - FRESH WATER   ....

YES / NO - BLACK WATER   ....

YES / NO - GREY WATER   ....

YES / NO - HARDSTANDING   ....

YES / NO - GRASS   ....

YES / NO - WI-FI   ....

NOTES

....
....
....
....
....
....
....
....
....
....
....
....

MY 100 FAVOURITE
GERMAN STELLPLATZ

DATE .... ARRIVAL TIME ....

AIRE NAME ....

ADDRESS 1 ....

ADDRESS 2 ....

REGION ....

WHAT3WORDS ///...

GPS ....

COST PER NIGHT € .... RECOMMEND - YES / NO

NO. OF NIGHTS HERE .... WEATHER ....

FACILITIES   THINGS TO SEE / DO LOCALLY

YES / NO - ELECTRICITY   ....
                              ....
YES / NO - FRESH WATER   ....
                              ....
YES / NO - BLACK WATER   ....
                              ....
YES / NO - GREY WATER   ....
                              ....
YES / NO - HARDSTANDING   ....
                              ....
YES / NO - GRASS   ....
                              ....
YES / NO - WI-FI   ....

NOTES

....
....
....
....
....
....
....
....
....
....
....

MY 100 FAVOURITE
GERMAN STELLPLATZ

DATE .... ARRIVAL TIME ....

AIRE NAME ....

ADDRESS 1 ....

ADDRESS 2 ....

REGION ....

WHAT3WORDS ///...

GPS ....

COST PER NIGHT € .... RECOMMEND – YES / NO

NO. OF NIGHTS HERE .... WEATHER ....

FACILITIES   THINGS TO SEE / DO LOCALLY

YES / NO - ELECTRICITY   ....

                              ....
YES / NO - FRESH WATER   ....

                              ....
YES / NO - BLACK WATER   ....

                              ....
YES / NO - GREY WATER   ....

                              ....
YES / NO - HARDSTANDING   ....

                              ....
YES / NO - GRASS   ....

                              ....
YES / NO - WI-FI   ....

NOTES

....
....
....
....
....
....
....
....
....
....
....

MY 100 FAVOURITE GERMAN STELLPLATZ

DATE .... ARRIVAL TIME ....

AIRE NAME ....

ADDRESS 1 ....

ADDRESS 2 ....

REGION ....

WHAT3WORDS ///...

GPS ....

COST PER NIGHT € .... RECOMMEND – YES / NO

NO. OF NIGHTS HERE .... WEATHER ....

FACILITIES

YES / NO – ELECTRICITY

YES / NO – FRESH WATER

YES / NO – BLACK WATER

YES / NO – GREY WATER

YES / NO – HARDSTANDING

YES / NO – GRASS

YES / NO – WI-FI

THINGS TO SEE / DO LOCALLY

....
....
....
....
....
....
....
....
....
....
....
....

NOTES

....
....
....
....
....
....
....
....
....
....
....

MY 100 FAVOURITE
GERMAN STELLPLATZ

DATE .... ARRIVAL TIME ....

AIRE NAME ....

ADDRESS 1 ....

ADDRESS 2 ....

REGION ....

WHAT3WORDS ///..

GPS ....

COST PER NIGHT € .... RECOMMEND – YES / NO

NO. OF NIGHTS HERE .... WEATHER ....

FACILITIES   THINGS TO SEE / DO LOCALLY

YES / NO – ELECTRICITY   ....

YES / NO – FRESH WATER   ....

YES / NO – BLACK WATER   ....

YES / NO – GREY WATER   ....

YES / NO – HARDSTANDING   ....

YES / NO – GRASS   ....

YES / NO – WI-FI   ....

NOTES

....
....
....
....
....
....
....
....
....
....
....

MY 100 FAVOURITE
GERMAN STELLPLATZ

DATE .... ARRIVAL TIME ....

AIRE NAME ....

ADDRESS 1 ....

ADDRESS 2 ....

REGION ....

WHAT3WORDS ///..

GPS ....

COST PER NIGHT € .... RECOMMEND – YES / NO

NO. OF NIGHTS HERE .... WEATHER ....

FACILITIES

YES / NO - ELECTRICITY

YES / NO - FRESH WATER

YES / NO - BLACK WATER

YES / NO - GREY WATER

YES / NO - HARDSTANDING

YES / NO - GRASS

YES / NO - WI-FI

THINGS TO SEE / DO LOCALLY

....
....
....
....
....
....
....
....
....
....

NOTES

....
....
....
....
....
....
....
....
....
....
....

MY 100 FAVOURITE
GERMAN STELLPLATZ

DATE .... ARRIVAL TIME ....

AIRE NAME ....

ADDRESS 1 ....

ADDRESS 2 ....

REGION ....

WHAT3WORDS ///...

GPS ....

COST PER NIGHT € .... RECOMMEND - YES / NO

NO. OF NIGHTS HERE .... WEATHER ....

FACILITIES   THINGS TO SEE / DO LOCALLY

YES / NO - ELECTRICITY   ....
                              ....
YES / NO - FRESH WATER   ....
                              ....
YES / NO - BLACK WATER   ....
                              ....
YES / NO - GREY WATER   ....
                              ....
YES / NO - HARDSTANDING   ....
                              ....
YES / NO - GRASS   ....
                              ....
YES / NO - WI-FI   ....

NOTES

....
....
....
....
....
....
....
....
....
....
....
....

MY 100 FAVOURITE
GERMAN STELLPLATZ

DATE .... ARRIVAL TIME ....

AIRE NAME ....

ADDRESS 1 ....

ADDRESS 2 ....

REGION ....

WHAT3WORDS ///...

GPS ....

COST PER NIGHT € .... RECOMMEND – YES / NO

NO. OF NIGHTS HERE .... WEATHER ....

FACILITIES   THINGS TO SEE / DO LOCALLY

YES / NO – ELECTRICITY   ....

                                ....
YES / NO – FRESH WATER   ....

                                ....
YES / NO – BLACK WATER   ....

                                ....
YES / NO – GREY WATER   ....

                                ....
YES / NO – HARDSTANDING   ....

                                ....
YES / NO – GRASS   ....

                                ....
YES / NO – WI-FI   ....

                            NOTES

....
....
....
....
....
....
....
....
....
....

MY 100 FAVOURITE
GERMAN STELLPLATZ

DATE .... ARRIVAL TIME ....

AIRE NAME ....

ADDRESS 1 ....

ADDRESS 2 ....

REGION ....

WHAT3WORDS ///...

GPS ....

COST PER NIGHT € .... RECOMMEND – YES / NO

NO. OF NIGHTS HERE .... WEATHER ....

FACILITIES   THINGS TO SEE / DO LOCALLY

YES / NO - ELECTRICITY ....

YES / NO - FRESH WATER ....

YES / NO - BLACK WATER ....

YES / NO - GREY WATER ....

YES / NO - HARDSTANDING ....

YES / NO - GRASS ....

YES / NO - WI-FI ....

NOTES

....
....
....
....
....
....
....
....
....
....

MY 100 FAVOURITE
GERMAN STELLPLATZ

DATE .... ARRIVAL TIME ....

AIRE NAME ....

ADDRESS 1 ....

ADDRESS 2 ....

REGION ....

WHAT3WORDS ///...

GPS ....

COST PER NIGHT € .... RECOMMEND – YES / NO

NO. OF NIGHTS HERE .... WEATHER ....

FACILITIES   THINGS TO SEE / DO LOCALLY

YES / NO – ELECTRICITY   ....
                              ....
YES / NO – FRESH WATER   ....
                              ....
YES / NO – BLACK WATER   ....
                              ....
YES / NO – GREY WATER   ....
                              ....
YES / NO – HARDSTANDING   ....
                              ....
YES / NO – GRASS   ....
                              ....
YES / NO – WI-FI   ....

NOTES

....
....
....
....
....
....
....
....
....
....
....

MY 100 FAVOURITE
GERMAN STELLPLATZ

DATE .... ARRIVAL TIME ....

AIRE NAME ....

ADDRESS 1 ....

ADDRESS 2 ....

REGION ....

WHAT3WORDS ///..

GPS ....

COST PER NIGHT € .... RECOMMEND – YES / NO

NO. OF NIGHTS HERE .... WEATHER ....

FACILITIES   THINGS TO SEE / DO LOCALLY

YES / NO – ELECTRICITY   ....
                            ....
YES / NO – FRESH WATER   ....
                            ....
YES / NO – BLACK WATER   ....
                            ....
YES / NO – GREY WATER   ....
                            ....
YES / NO – HARDSTANDING   ....
                            ....
YES / NO – GRASS   ....
                            ....
YES / NO – WI-FI   ....

NOTES

....
....
....
....
....
....
....
....
....
....

MY 100 FAVOURITE
GERMAN STELLPLATZ

DATE .... ARRIVAL TIME ....

AIRE NAME ....

ADDRESS 1 ....

ADDRESS 2 ....

REGION ....

WHAT3WORDS ///...

GPS ....

COST PER NIGHT € .... RECOMMEND - YES / NO

NO. OF NIGHTS HERE .... WEATHER ....

FACILITIES   THINGS TO SEE / DO LOCALLY

YES / NO - ELECTRICITY   ....
                              ....
YES / NO - FRESH WATER   ....
                              ....
YES / NO - BLACK WATER   ....
                              ....
YES / NO - GREY WATER   ....
                              ....
YES / NO - HARDSTANDING   ....
                              ....
YES / NO - GRASS   ....
                              ....
YES / NO - WI-FI   ....

NOTES

....
....
....
....
....
....
....
....
....
....
....
....

MY 100 FAVOURITE GERMAN STELLPLATZ

LIST OF STELLPLATZ

1 ....

2 ....

3 ....

4 ....

5 ....

6 ....

7 ....

8 ....

9 ....

10 ....

11 ....

12 ....

13 ....

14 ....

15 ....

16 ....

17 ....

18 ....

19 ....

20 ....

21 ....

22 ....

23 ....

24 ....

25 ....

MY 100 FAVOURITE
GERMAN STELLPLATZ

LIST OF STELLPLATZ

26 ....

27 ....

28 ....

29 ....

30 ....

31 ....

32 ....

33 ....

34 ....

35 ....

36 ....

37 ....

38 ....

39 ....

40 ....

41 ....

42 ....

43 ....

44 ....

45 ....

46 ....

47 ....

48 ....

49 ....

50 ....

MY 100 FAVOURITE
GERMAN STELLPLATZ

LIST OF STELLPLATZ

51 ....

52 ....

53 ....

54 ....

55 ....

56 ....

57 ....

58 ....

59 ....

60 ....

61 ....

62 ....

63 ....

64 ....

65 ....

66 ....

67 ....

68 ....

69 ....

70 ....

71 ....

72 ....

73 ....

74 ....

75 ....

MY 100 FAVOURITE
GERMAN STELLPLATZ

LIST OF STELLPLATZ

76 ....

77 ....

78 ....

79 ....

80 ....

81 ....

82 ....

83 ....

84 ....

85 ....

86 ....

87 ....

88 ....

89 ....

90 ....

91 ....

92 ....

93 ....

94 ....

95 ....

96 ....

97 ....

98 ....

99 ....

100 ....